MW01006377

THE BOOK OF CAMPING KNOTS

For those two
calamity campers
Jacky and Olivia

THE BOOK OF
CAMPING KNOTS

PETER OWEN

THE LYONS PRESS
Guilford, Connecticut
An imprint of The Globe Pequot Press

To buy books in quantity for corporate use
or incentives, call **(800) 962–0973**
or e-mail **premiums@GlobePequot.com.**

Copyright © 2000 by Peter Owen

All rights reserved. No part of this book may be reproduced or
transmitted in any form by any means, electronic or mechanical,
including photocopying and recording, or by any information
storage and retrieval system, except as may be expressly
permitted by the 1976 Copyright Act or by the publisher.
Requests for permission should be made in writing to The Globe
Pequot Press, P.O. Box 480, Guilford, Connecticut 06437.

The Lyons Press is an imprint of The Globe Pequot Press

Designed and illustrated by Peter Owen

Library of Congress Cataloging-in-Publication Data is available on
file.

ISBN 978-1-55821-927-4

Printed in Canada

10 9 8 7 6 5 4 3

CONTENTS

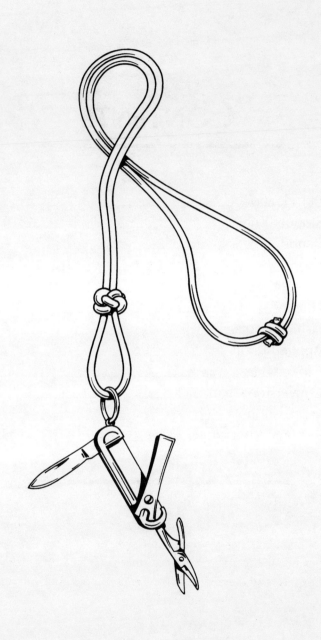

INTRODUCTION

Camping, like many outdoor activities, has undergone some revolutionary changes in recent years. Many more people now have the free recreational time and the access to spend time camping, backpacking, and exploring wild areas. But undoubtably one of the biggest changes has been in the equipment that is now available to anyone who wants to venture into the outdoors. The highly developed camping equipment and apparel of today is, in the main, manufactured or constructed from the very latest high-tech, light-weight materials. All ropes and cords are now made from artificial or synthetic materials. There is a vast range of "camping gadgets" available to cope with almost anything that you will need to survive in the outdoors. Arguably the only components that have changed very little over recent years, but are still absolutely essential, are the range of knots that all campers should know.

The Book of Camping Knots gives you the opportunity to master 30 classic camping knots. In focusing solely on the knots, each knot is allocated generous space for clear instructions and meticulous step-by-step illustrations.

The knots are divided into several distinct groups, each of which is used for different purposes. Practice is essential for good knot tying, so select the right knot for the job and practice until you are confident that you can tie it quickly, securely, and literally with your eyes closed. Your survival in the outdoors may depend on it!

CAMPING KNOTS

Given the type and range of camping equipment available today, it is quite possible to go on a camping expedition and not have to tie a single knot. On the other hand it is in those difficult moments of having to solve a problem that knowing the right knot to tie can literally be a life saver!

Many of the knots illustrated in this book have several uses and can be adapted to solve different problems. A common problem that campers can face is securing tent guylines on ground that is too hard or rocky to use pegs. The high-tech, self-erecting tent that you have bought may be an excellent tent, but unless you can properly secure it in extreme weather conditions it is not going to be an effective shelter. In this type of situation tie additional guylines from the top of the tent poles to large rocks situated around the tent, the best knots to use for this purpose are hitches (see page 69).

A more serious example of knowing how to tie the correct knots is if you find yourself in an emergency situation and you need to build a shelter to protect you from the wind, rain or sun. Improvised shelters tend to be flimsy so the knots that hold the branches, foliage, or anything else you may use, together, need to be secure. An excellent knot for this purpose is the transom knot (see page 80).

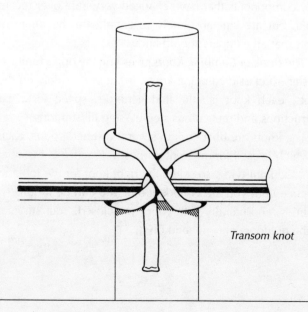

Transom knot

ROPES

Rope is manufactured in either natural or artificial fibers that can be twisted or braided and is available in a wide variety of sizes. Rope size can be measured by circumference or diameter or by a term; for example, "twine," tells you that it is a thin line for various uses.

Traditionally, rope was made by twisting fibers of natural materials together. The most commonly used materials were manila, sisal, coir, hemp, flax, and cotton. The fibers were twisted first into yarn, then into strands, and finally into rope, in a process called laying up. This type of rope is refered to as hawser-laid.

Artificial or synthetic materials have almost completely replaced natural fibers in the manufacture of rope for outdoor use. Man-made filaments can be spun to run the whole length of a line, do not vary in thickness, and do not have to be twisted together to make them cohere. This gives them superior strength.

Nylon, first produced in 1938 for domestic use, was the first man-made material to be used in this way. Since then a range of artificial ropes has been developed to meet different purposes, but they all share certain characteristics. Size for size they are lighter, stronger, and cheaper than their natural counterparts. They do not rot or mildew, are resistant to sunlight, chemicals, oil, gasoline, and most common solvents. They can also be made in a range of colors. Color-coded ropes make for instant recognition of lines of different function and size.

The vast majority of rope in use today, is kernmantle rope (see page 11). It is easy to handle, very flexible and has a good strength-to-weight ratio. Older style hawser-laid nylon rope (see page 10), is still widely used for general camping purposes or where cost is a consideration.

Rope manufactured from artificial fiber, does have some disadvantages, the main one being that they melt when heated. Even the friction generated when one rope rubs against another may be enough to cause damage, so it is vital to check your ropes regularly. It is also possible for heat friction to fuse knotted rope together so that it is impossible to untie the knot. Another disadvantage is that artificial ropes made of continuous filaments are so smooth that knots slip and come undone. Knots may need to be secured with additional knots.

HAWSER-LAID ROPE

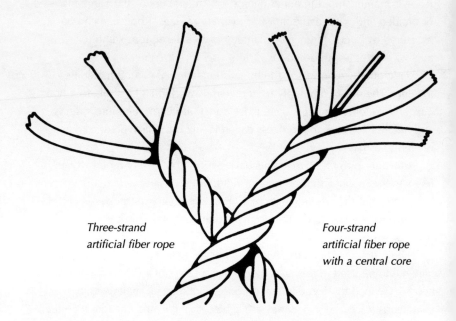

*Three-strand
artificial fiber rope*

*Four-strand
artificial fiber rope
with a central core*

Artificial rope can be laid up or twisted like old-style natural fiber rope. This is known as hawser-laid. Usually three strands of nylon filaments are twisted together to form the rope. There are variations of this available: One very strong variation is four strands of nylon filament twisted around a central nylon core.

The cost of hawser-laid rope is generally about two thirds that of the more widely used kernmantle constructed rope. Laid-up rope, made of thick multifilaments tightly twisted together, may be very resistant to wear, but it may also be difficult to handle because of its stiffness and knots may not hold well. As a general rule, do not buy a rope that is too stiff. Similarly, be wary of twisted rope that is very soft.

This type of rope may be perfectly acceptable for general camping purposes but should be avoided in situations where a rope will be subject to any excesive forms of strain.

KERNMANTLE ROPE

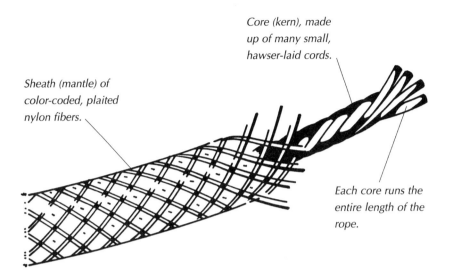

Core (kern), made
up of many small,
hawser-laid cords.

Sheath (mantle) of
color-coded, plaited
nylon fibers.

Each core runs the
entire length of the
rope.

Kernmantle rope is made from synthetic materials, having a core, or "kern,"
of many small, hawser-laid cords contained in a braided sheath, or "mantle."
Kernmantle rope is very strong while being extremely flexible and easy to
handle. Its flexibility makes it ideal for knot tying and the smoothness of the
outer sheath not only makes the rope easy and comfortable to handle but it
also allows for good contact and easy use with a block and pulley or
climbing equipment such as karabiners and belay devices.

Some kernmantle ropes are sold featuring various dry treatments. These
are highly recommended for use in wet or icy conditions. It means that the
rope has been chemically treated to repel water. Kernmantle ropes are likely
to absorb upwards of 20 percent of their weight in water when used in wet
and icy conditions. The disadvantages of this are first, the rope weighs a lot
more, counteracting the light-weight qualities of kernmantle, and second,
and most crucial, the rope looses strength, possibly as much as 40 percent.
Dry treatment will also prevent dirt particles from working their way into the
fibers of the rope and causing damage.

LOOKING AFTER ROPE

Rope is sturdy material, but it is expensive, so it's worth looking after it properly. Caring for rope will help it keep its strength and prolong its life. Avoid dragging it over rough, sharp edges, or dirty, gritty surfaces where particles could get into the rope and damage it. Do not walk on rope or force it into harsh kinks. Inspect it regularly and wash off dirt, grit, and oil. Coil rope carefully and always make sure it is dry before coiling, even if it is artificial fiber rope. If it has been in seawater, rinse thoroughly to remove all salt deposits.

If knots are repeatedly tied in one section of rope, that section will weaken. The tighter the nip or the sharper the curve the greater the chances that the rope will break; if it does, it will part immediately outside the knot.

Finally, never use two ropes of different material together, because only the more rigid of the two will work under strain.

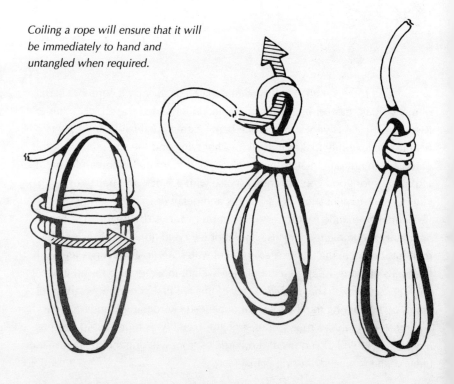

Coiling a rope will ensure that it will be immediately to hand and untangled when required.

TYING FISHING KNOTS

Fishing line is made from strong, flexible monofilament nylon and tying effective knots in this type of material requires a few routine maneuvers to be followed. Instructions for tying the most commonly used fishing knots can be found, starting on page 105.

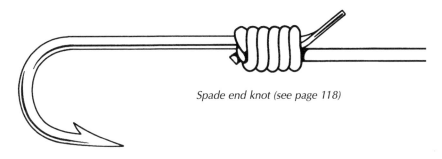

Spade end knot (see page 118)

Tying fishing knots with monofilament nylon:

• Before tying any knot always check the line for any visible signs of damage. If in any doubt, safely discard that section of line.

• To reduce friction and to help the knot seat correctly, lubricate it with saliva or water before drawing it together.

• Draw the knot together slowly and evenly with a minimum of friction to ensure it seats correctly.

• Continue to draw the knot together as tight as possible. A knot will begin to slip just before it breaks—so the tighter it is drawn together, the more force it can withstand before it starts to slip.

• Once the knot has been tightened as much as possible and is seated correctly, trim the knot ends. This will avoid them catching on rod rings, hooks, or weeds.

• Visually check your knot—good knots look good. If you are not fully confident that the knot has been tied and seated correctly—don't gamble! Cut it off and retie it.

• As with all knots, practice tying your fishing knots at home until they become second nature.You will find that you can rely on a small number of knots to cover most types of fishing, but it is important to be able to tie those knots quickly and with full confidence.

How to Use This Book

The diagrams accompanying the descriptions of the knots are intended to be self-explanatory, but for added clarity, sequenced, written instructions and special tying techniques and methods do accompany the knots. There are arrows to show the directions in which you should push or pull the working ends and standing parts of the rope or line. The dotted lines indicate intermediate positions of the rope. When tying a knot you should always have a sufficient working end to complete it. The amount of working end required can often be calculated by looking at the illustration of the finished knot. Always follow the order shown of going over or under a length of line; reversing or changing this order could result in a completely different knot, which might well be unstable, unsafe, and insecure.

ROPE PARTS

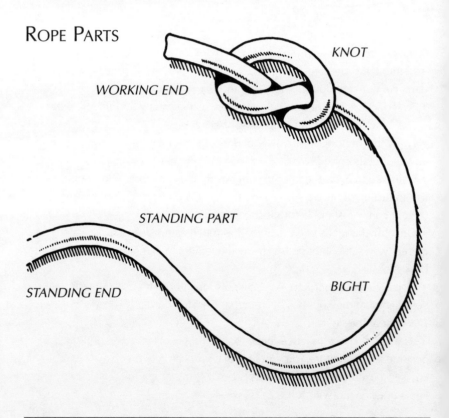

KNOT

WORKING END

STANDING PART

STANDING END

BIGHT

PLEASE...

Respect the great outdoors. When you have left your campsite it should look as if you had never been there. Take all your rubbish away with you—concealing it is not acceptable. The great outdoors must remain unspoiled so that future generations of visitors can enjoy it in the same way that you have.

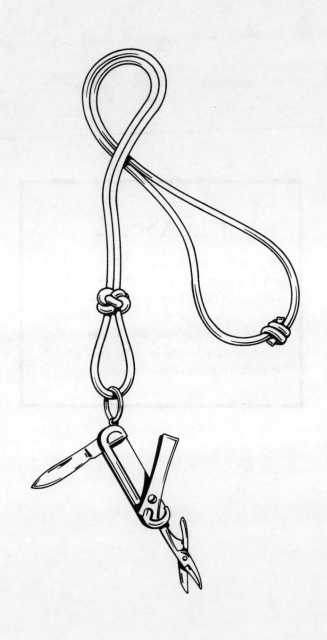

STOPPER KNOTS

S topper knots, as their name suggests, are used to prevent the end of a rope or line from slipping through an eye, loop, or hole. They can be used to bind the end of a rope so that it will not unravel or weight the end of a rope for throwing purposes and for decoration.

Many camping knots, for example, the bowline (see page 50) can be finished off with a stopper knot tied in the working end for extra security.

OVERHAND KNOT

Also known as the thumb knot, this knot forms the basis for many others. It is used in its own right as a stopper knot and makes a line easier to grip if tied at regular intervals along the line. A tight overhand knot can be difficult to undo if tied in very small-diameter line or if the line becomes wet.

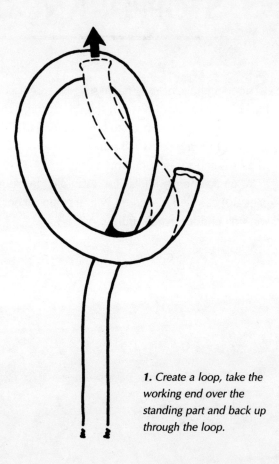

1. Create a loop, take the working end over the standing part and back up through the loop.

2. Pull on the working end and the standing part to form the final knot.

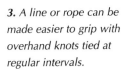

3. A line or rope can be made easier to grip with overhand knots tied at regular intervals.

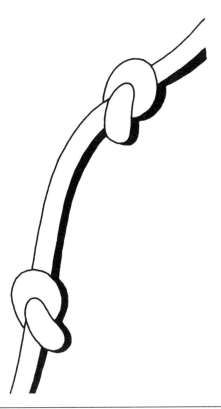

FIGURE-EIGHT KNOT

This is a quick and efficient way of tying a simple and attractive stopper knot at the end a line or rope. The knot's name comes from its characteristic shape. Its interlaced appearance has long been seen as a symbol of interwoven affection. In heraldry it signifies faithful love and appears on various coats of arms—hence its other names, the Flemish or Savoy knot.

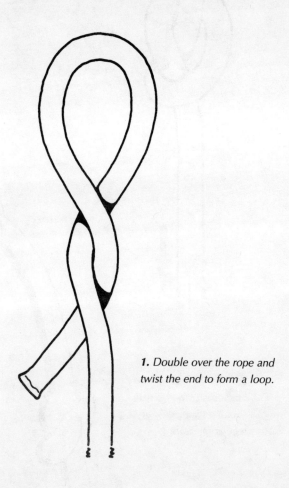

1. Double over the rope and twist the end to form a loop.

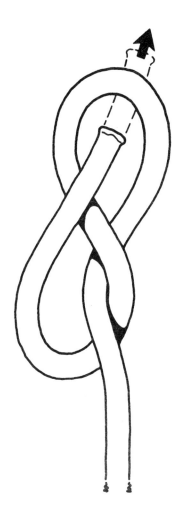

2. Pass the working end over the standing part and then up through the loop.

3. Pull on both the working end and the standing part to form the knot.

HEAVING LINE KNOT

This stopper knot has the advantage of adding considerable weight to the end of the line. This proves particularly useful for throwing the end of a line across a gap or to another person.

The heaving line knot, widely used by sailors, is tied at the end of a lighter line which in turn is attached to a heavier line. The lighter line is thrown first, usually from boat to shore, so the heavier line can then be drawn or heaved behind it.

The knot's other name, the monk's knot, derives from its use by Franciscan monks to weight the ends of the cords they use as belts.

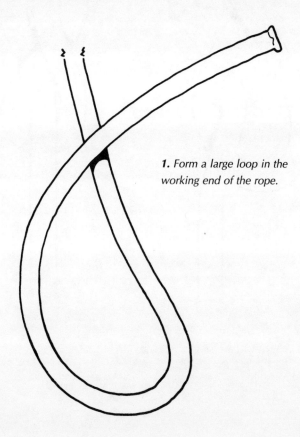

1. Form a large loop in the working end of the rope.

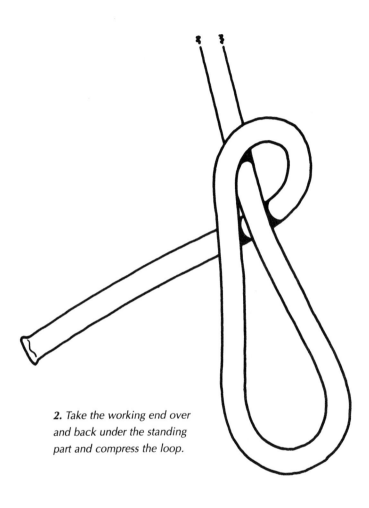

2. Take the working end over and back under the standing part and compress the loop.

continued on page 24

Heaving Line Knot

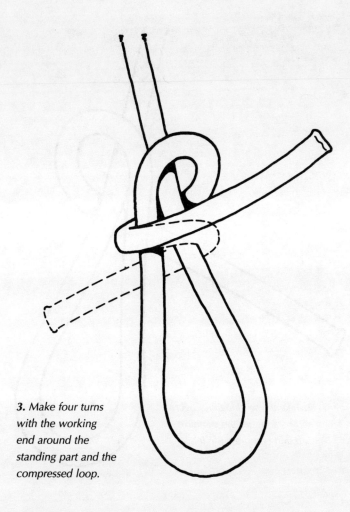

3. *Make four turns with the working end around the standing part and the compressed loop.*

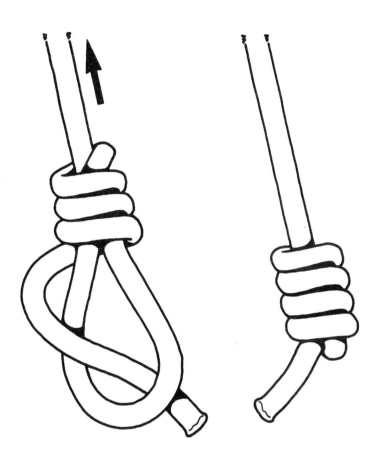

4. On the fourth turn take the working end down through the loop. Keep the already formed turns as tight as possible.

5. Pull on the working end and the standing part to tighten the knot. As the knot is tightening, form the final knot shape.

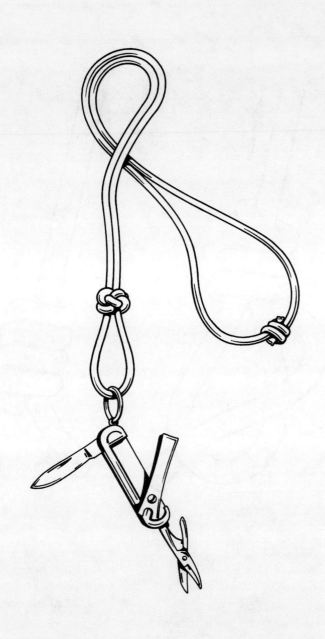

BENDS

B ends are used to join two lengths of rope at their ends to form one longer piece. It is important, if bends are to be secure, for the ropes joined in this way to be of the same kind and the same diameter.

The sheet bend (see page 32) is the exception to this rule. It is very secure, even when it is used to join ropes of different diameters.

REEF KNOT

The reef knot, or square knot, is very often the only knot people know, apart from the granny knot. It gets its name from its nautical use to tie two ends of a rope when reefing or gathering in part of a sail.

The reef knot is not a secure knot and should not be used as one, certainly never with ropes of different diameter. It should only be used to make a temporary join in lines of identical type, weight, and diameter where it will not be put under strain. If the lines have to take strain, stopper knots should be tied in the short ends.

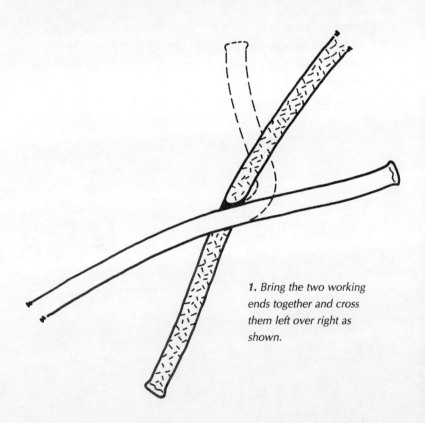

1. Bring the two working ends together and cross them left over right as shown.

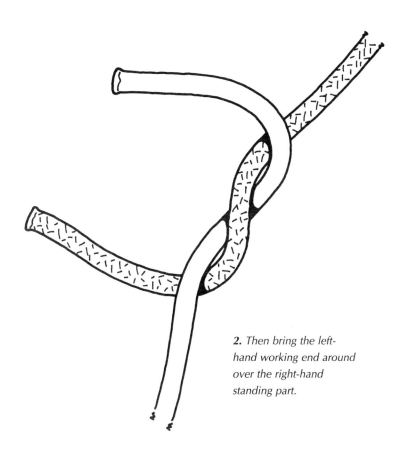

2. Then bring the left-hand working end around over the right-hand standing part.

continued on page 30

Reef Knot

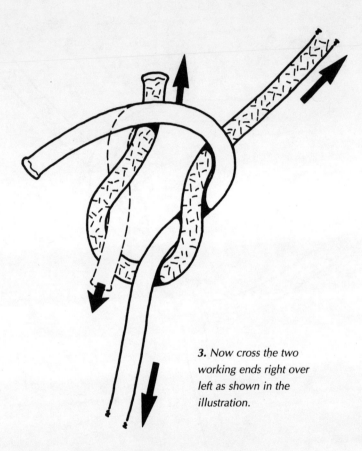

3. Now cross the two working ends right over left as shown in the illustration.

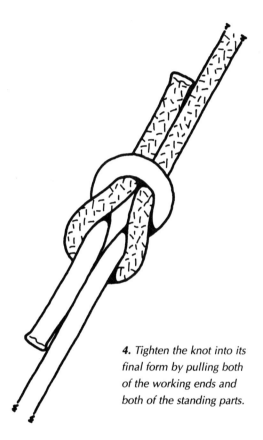

4. Tighten the knot into its
final form by pulling both
of the working ends and
both of the standing parts.

SHEET BEND

The sheet bend is probably the most commonly used of all bends and, unlike most bends, it can safely join lines of different diameters. It is not, however, one hundred percent secure and should never be used in circumstances where it will be subject to great strain. Its breaking strength also decreases in direct proportion to the difference in diameter of the lines joined.

A slipped sheet bend is formed by placing a bight between the loop of the heavier rope and the standing part of the lighter one. The slipped knot is more easily untied when the rope is under strain.

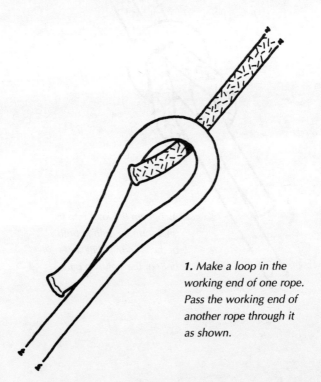

1. Make a loop in the working end of one rope. Pass the working end of another rope through it as shown.

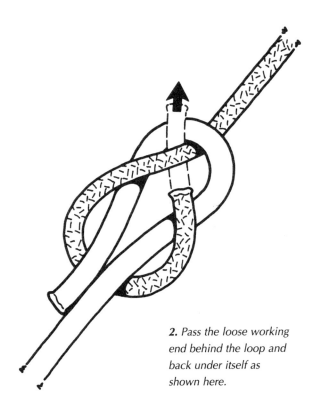

2. Pass the loose working
end behind the loop and
back under itself as
shown here.

continued on page 34

Sheet Bend

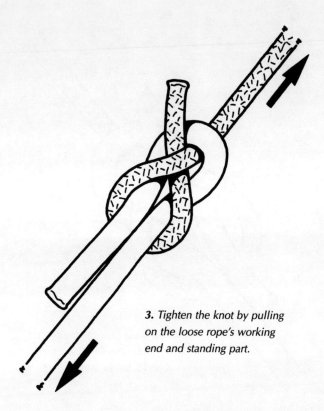

3. Tighten the knot by pulling
on the loose rope's working
end and standing part.

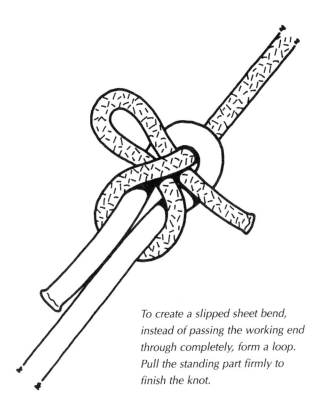

To create a slipped sheet bend,
instead of passing the working end
through completely, form a loop.
Pull the standing part firmly to
finish the knot.

FISHERMAN'S KNOT

This knot is said to have been invented in the nineteenth century, but some authorities suggest it was known to the ancient Greeks. It is generally known as the fisherman's knot, but over the years it has picked up many different names (angler's knot, English knot, Englishman's bend, halibut knot, true lover's knot, and waterman's knot). It is formed from two overhand knots that jam against each other; the short ends are on opposite sides and lie almost parallel to their nearest standing part. After use, the two component knots are generally easily separated and undone.

The fisherman's knot is best suited to joining thin lines such as string, cord, twine, or small stuff, and as the name suggests, it is widely used by fishermen for joining the finest of fishing lines.

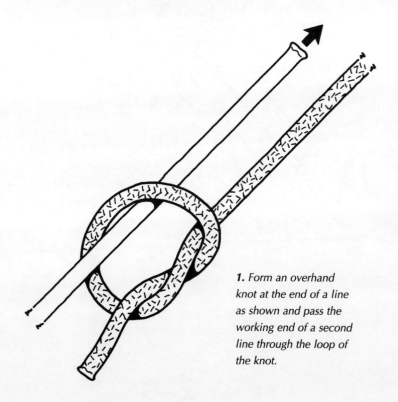

1. Form an overhand knot at the end of a line as shown and pass the working end of a second line through the loop of the knot.

2. Form the second overhand knot around the standing part of the first line as shown.

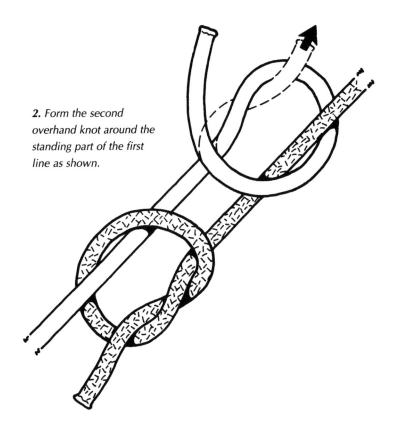

continued on page 38

Fisherman's Knot

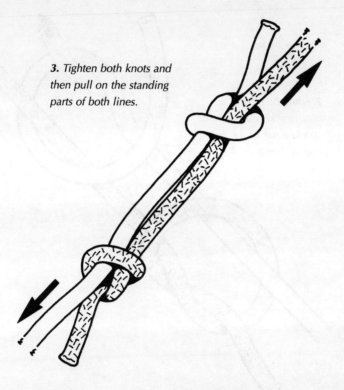

3. Tighten both knots and then pull on the standing parts of both lines.

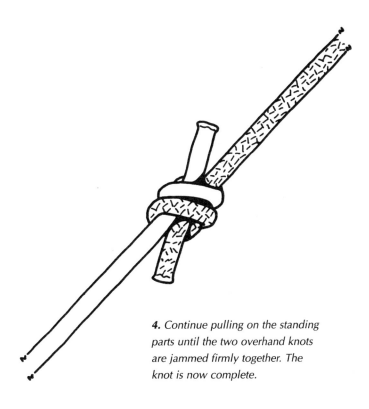

4. *Continue pulling on the standing parts until the two overhand knots are jammed firmly together. The knot is now complete.*

FIGURE-EIGHT BEND

This simple knot (also known as the Flemish bend or knot) is tied by making a figure-eight knot in one end of a line and then following it around with the other working end. It is, despite its simplicity, one of the strongest bends and holds equally well in cord or rope.

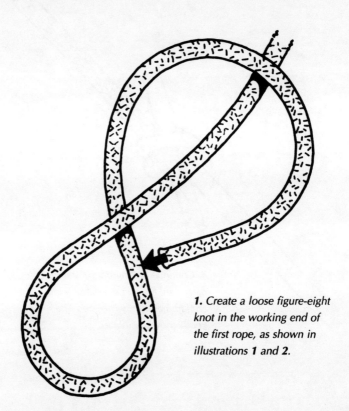

1. Create a loose figure-eight knot in the working end of the first rope, as shown in illustrations 1 and 2.

2. Do not pull the knot tight at this stage.

continued on page 42

Figure-Eight Bend

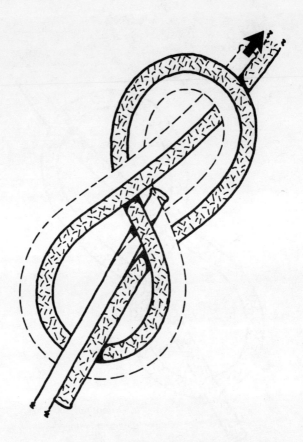

3. Feed the working end of the second rope into the loose figure-eight formed in the first rope and follow the figure-eight pattern around as shown in the illustration.

4. Tighten the knot into its final form by pulling on the standing part of each rope.

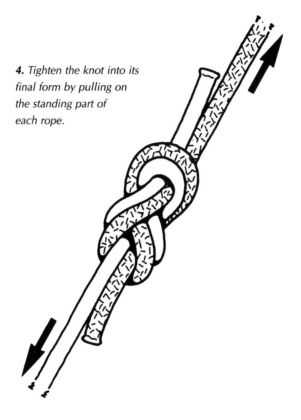

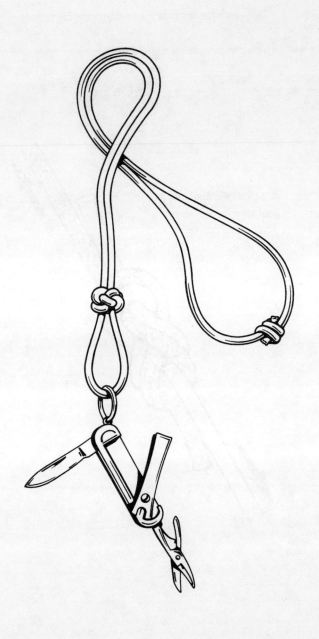

LOOPS

Knots made in the end of a rope by folding it back into an eye or loop and then knotting it to its own standing part are called loops. They are fixed and do not slide.

Loops are particularly important to campers, as they have such a wide variation of use. The figure-eight loop (see page 46), for example, is acknowledged as one of the quickest and most efficient ways to form a secure loop to drop over any object.

Figure-Eight Loop

This is one of the best-known and most widely used of all knots. It is probably the safest and quickest way to form a loop at the end of a rope.

It is comparatively easy to tie and it stays tied. Its disadvantages—it is difficult to adjust and cannot easily be untied after loading—tend to be outweighed by its general usefulness.

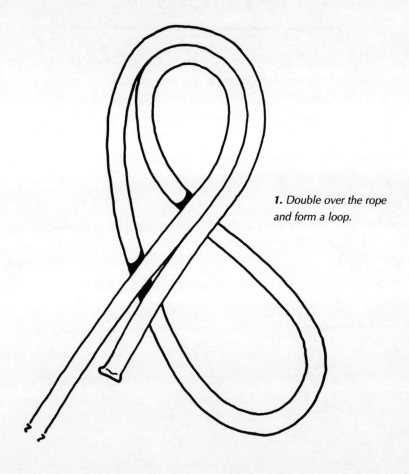

1. Double over the rope and form a loop.

2. Now bring the doubled working end over the doubled standing part and back up through the original loop.

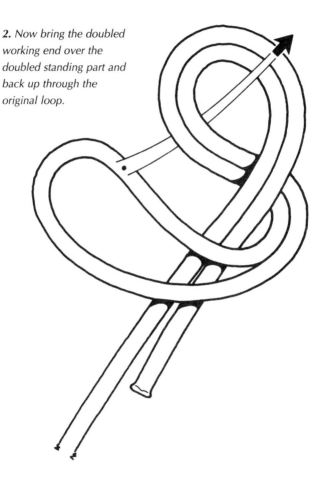

continued on page 48

Figure-Eight Loop

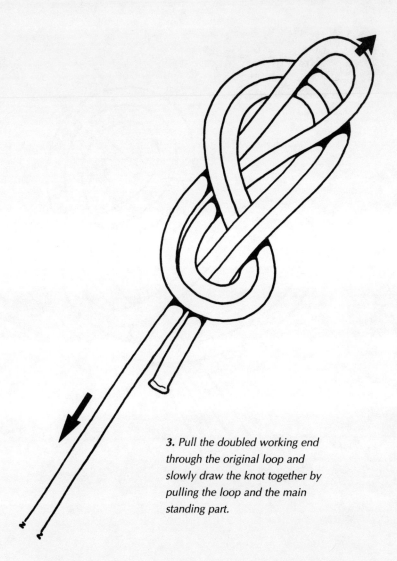

3. Pull the doubled working end
through the original loop and
slowly draw the knot together by
pulling the loop and the main
standing part.

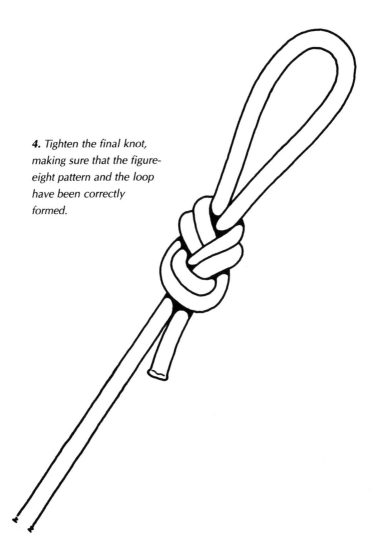

4. *Tighten the final knot, making sure that the figure-eight pattern and the loop have been correctly formed.*

BOWLINE

The bowline is one of the best-known and most widely used knots. It is tied to form a fixed loop at the end of a line or to attach a rope to an object.

The bowline's main advantages are that it does not slip, come loose, or jam. It is quick and easy to untie, even when a line is under tension, by pushing forward the bight that encircles the standing part of the line. For added security the bowline can be finished with a stopper knot.

1. Estimate the size of fixed loop required and create a small loop at that point in the standing part of the rope. Bring the working end of the rope back up and through the loop as shown in the illustration.

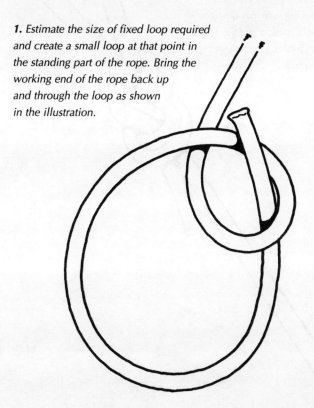

2. Take the working end around the back
of the standing part and back down
through the loop. Then slowly start
to pull on the standing part to
form the knot.

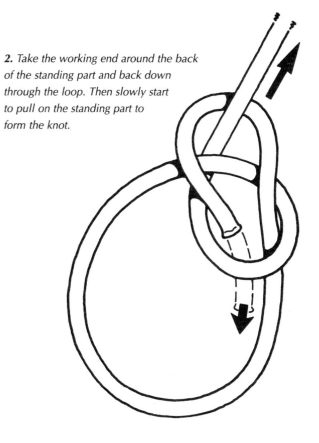

continued on page 52

Bowline

3. Adjust the fixed loop to its required size and then tighten the knot into its final form.

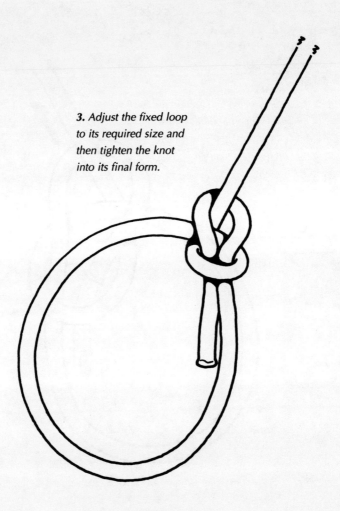

4. *For added security the bowline can be finished with a stopper knot.*

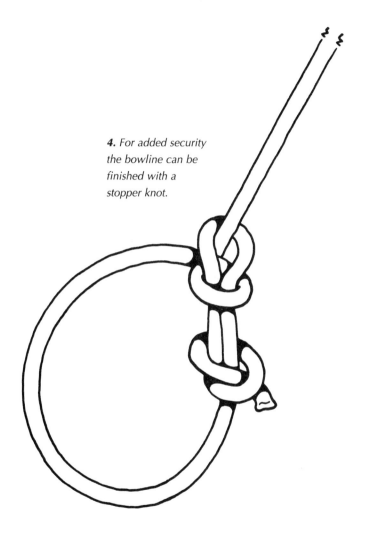

THREE-PART CROWN

This sturdy, secure knot can be used to hang food and gear and it can be used as a decorative knot from which to hang objects. It may become difficult to untie after it has supported a heavy weight.

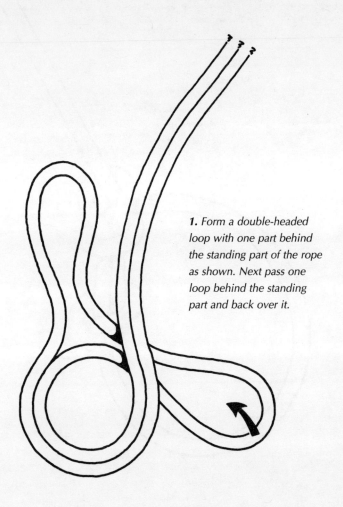

1. Form a double-headed loop with one part behind the standing part of the rope as shown. Next pass one loop behind the standing part and back over it.

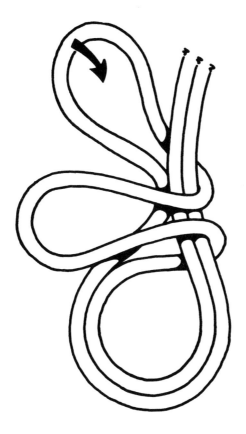

2. Keeping the first loop held firmly against the standing part, bring the second loop down over it toward the double loop.

continued on page 56

Three-Part Crown

3. *Pass the top loop through the double loop.*

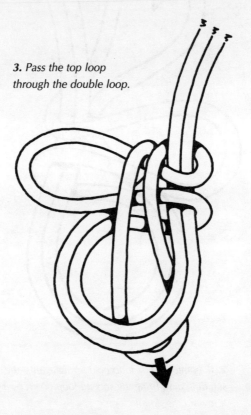

4. Finish the knot by pulling the standing part and the two loops. Take care to keep the two loops equal.

NOOSE

This simple knot is often used by campers and hunters to snare birds and small game such as rabbits. It can also be used in tying a parcel or, on a larger scale, it can be used to put tackle cables under stress.

The noose can be used as a hitch, especially if the hitch is to be formed around a very large object, such as a tree trunk, as a noose can be tied using a fairly short length of line. A constrictor knot, or a clove or cow hitch, would need a much longer length of rope. Also, a noose used as a hitch is very secure.

Another useful feature of the noose is that it can be tied around relatively inaccessible objects. A s long as it is possible to get close enough to pass a rope around, a noose can be tied and tightened.

A stopper knot should be added to the noose to prevent it from slipping.

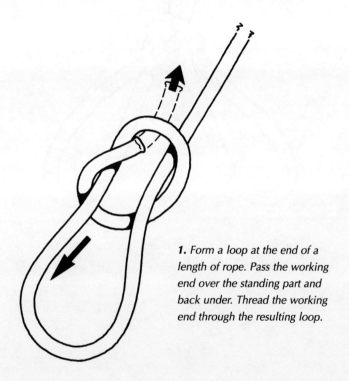

1. Form a loop at the end of a length of rope. Pass the working end over the standing part and back under. Thread the working end through the resulting loop.

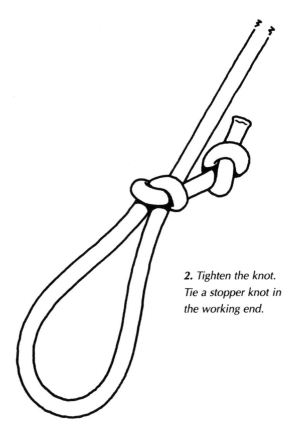

2. *Tighten the knot.*
Tie a stopper knot in
the working end.

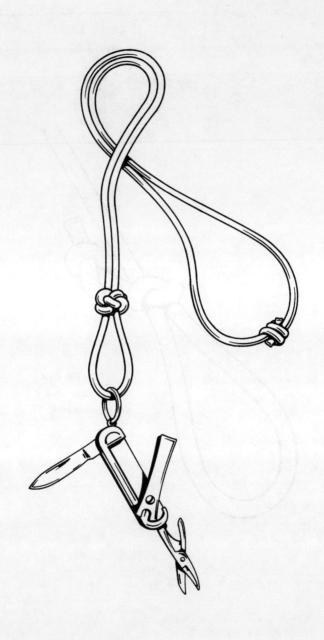

SHORTENINGS

Shortenings are invaluable knots well worth mastering. As their name suggests, they are used to shorten lengths of rope or line without cutting. A rope shortened by means of a knot can always be lengthened later, and a single unbroken line will always be more secure than two lines knotted together.

Shortenings can also be used as an emergency measure to take up damaged lengths of rope. The weakened sections are incorporated into the knot and are not, therefore, subject to strain.

SHEEPSHANK

The sheepshank can be used to shorten any rope to any required length without cutting. It is easy to tie, holds under tension with a good jamming action, does not change its shape, and unties easily.

In an emergency a sheepshank can be used to shorten a damaged line or rope, take care to ensure that the damaged or weakened section of the rope passes through both half hitches.

1. Form three loops at the point in the rope where the shortening will be required. Pull the indicated points of the middle loop through the two outer loops.

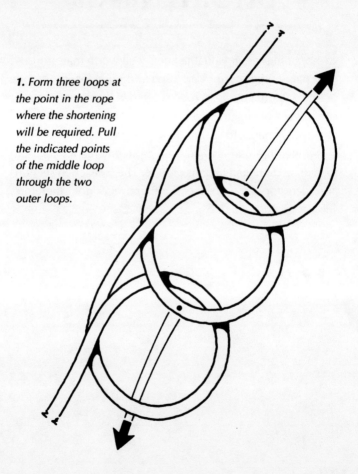

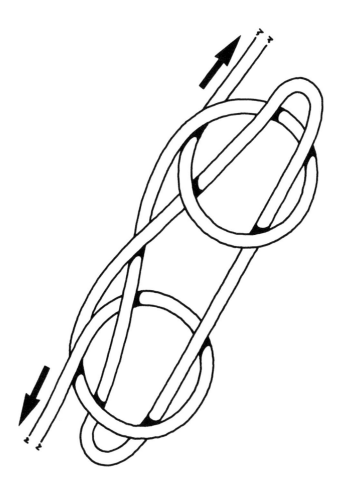

2. Slowly pull on the two main parts of the rope, making sure that the knot retains its shape and form.

continued on page 64

Sheepshank

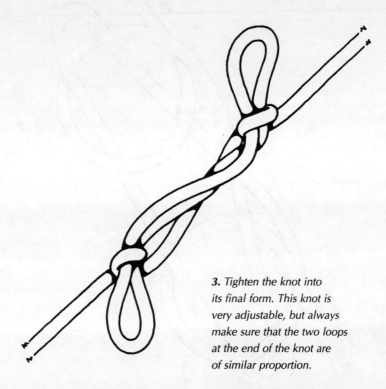

3. Tighten the knot into its final form. This knot is very adjustable, but always make sure that the two loops at the end of the knot are of similar proportion.

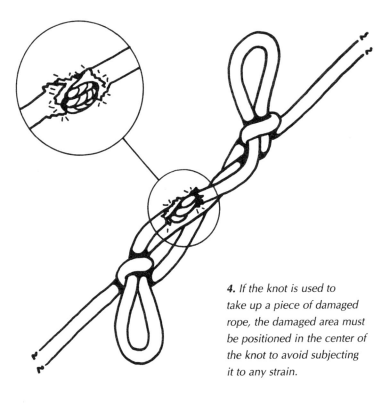

4. If the knot is used to take up a piece of damaged rope, the damaged area must be positioned in the center of the knot to avoid subjecting it to any strain.

LOOP KNOT

This is a very simple knot that can be used to form a quick and simple loop in a rope. More important, it can be used in an emergency to shorten a damaged rope. The weakened or damaged section of the rope is taken up in the center of the knot where it cannot be put under any strain.

The risks involved in using damaged or weakened rope for any outdoor activities are too great!

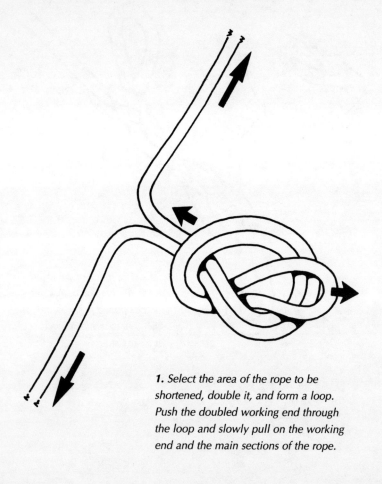

1. Select the area of the rope to be shortened, double it, and form a loop. Push the doubled working end through the loop and slowly pull on the working end and the main sections of the rope.

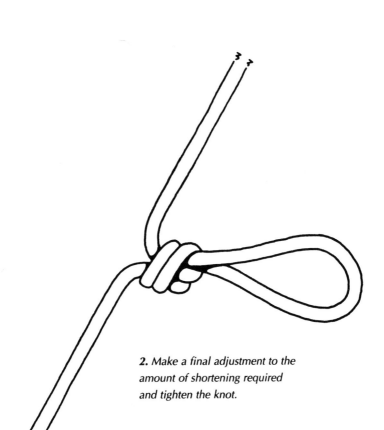

2. Make a final adjustment to the amount of shortening required and tighten the knot.

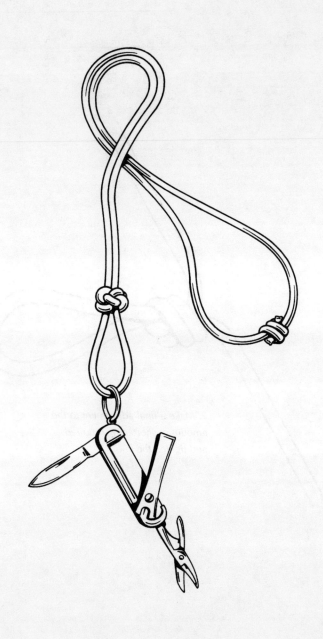

HITCHES

Hitches are knots used to secure a rope to another object (such as a post, peg, ring, luggage rack), or to fix together crossed pieces of rigid material, for example, building a shelter out of branches and foliage.

HALF HITCH

The half hitch is a very widely used fastening. It is, in fact, a single hitch formed around the standing part of another hitch. It is used to complete and strengthen other knots, as in the round turn and two half hitches (see page 88), which can then be used for tying, hanging, hooking objects etc. The slipped half hitch is a useful variation of the simple half hitch; a sharp pull on the working end releases the knot.

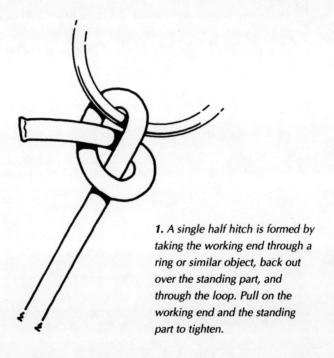

1. A single half hitch is formed by taking the working end through a ring or similar object, back out over the standing part, and through the loop. Pull on the working end and the standing part to tighten.

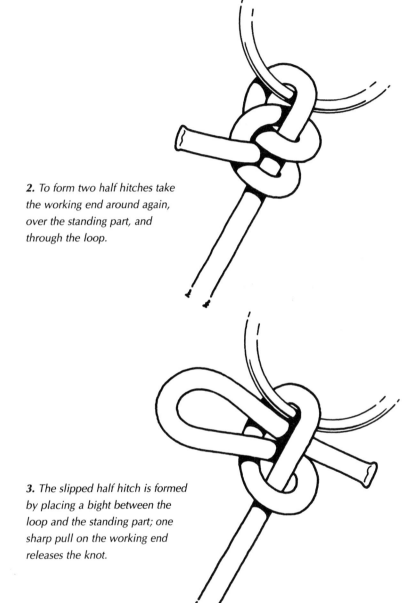

2. To form two half hitches take the working end around again, over the standing part, and through the loop.

3. The slipped half hitch is formed by placing a bight between the loop and the standing part; one sharp pull on the working end releases the knot.

Clove Hitch

The clove hitch is one of the best-known camping knots and probably one of the most valuable hitches. It can be used to fasten a line to a peg, pole, or post or on to another rope that is not part of the knot. It is an easy knot to tie, and can with practice be tied with just one hand. The final knot can be achieved in many different ways.

The clove hitch is not, however, a totally secure knot, as it will work loose if the strain is intermittent and comes from different angles. Under these types of conditions it is best used as a temporary hold, and then replaced by a more stable knot. It can be made more secure by adding a stopper knot to the working end.

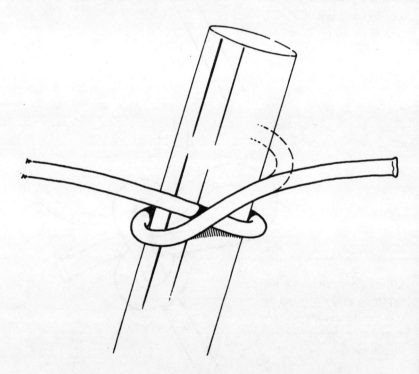

1. *Pass the working end around the peg, pole, or post and then cross it over the standing part before starting to pass it around again.*

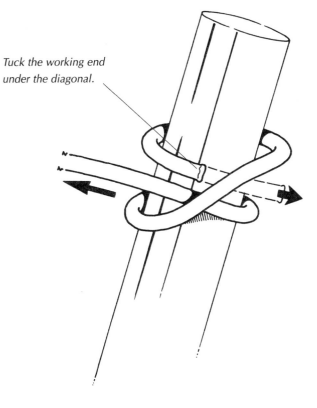

Tuck the working end
under the diagonal.

2. Bring the working end around above the first turn
and tuck it under the diagonal. Slowly start to pull
on the standing part.

continued on page 74

Clove Hitch

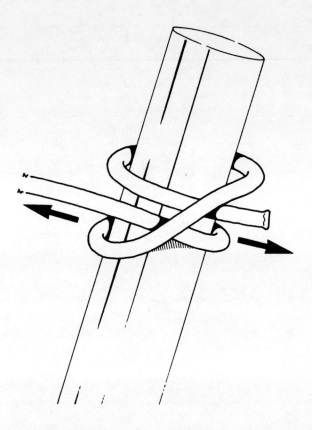

3. Slowly pull the working end and the standing part, making sure that the knot keeps its pattern and shape.

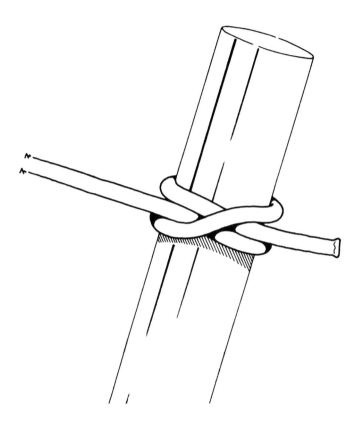

4. Tighten the knot into its final form.

CONSTRICTOR KNOT

This is a popular all-purpose knot because it is firm and does not slip. It can be used as a permanent or temporary fastening. As a permanent fastening, the constrictor knot grips so firmly that if there is a need to untie it, usually the only way is to cut it free. To be sure of being able to untie it if used as a temporary fastening, the last tuck should be made with a bight to make a slip knot.

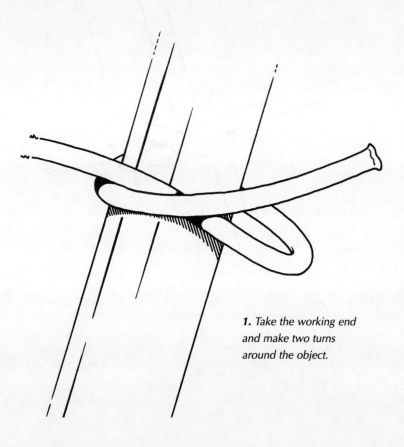

1. Take the working end and make two turns around the object.

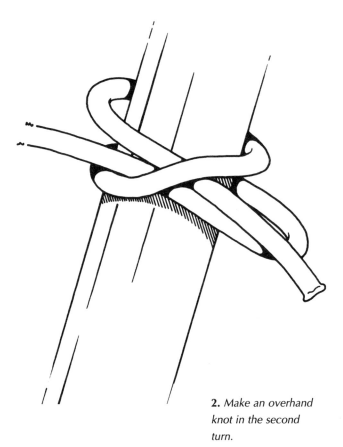

2. *Make an overhand knot in the second turn.*

continued on page 78

Constrictor Knot

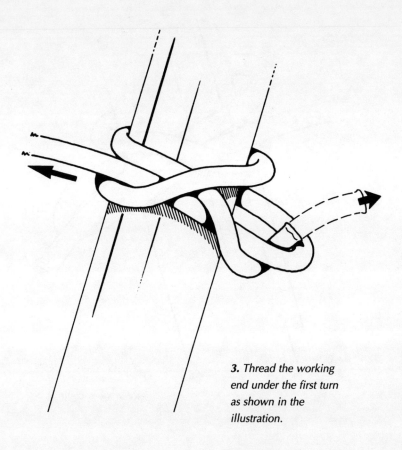

3. Thread the working end under the first turn as shown in the illustration.

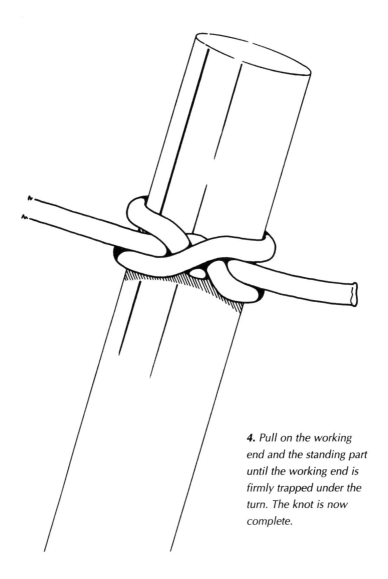

4. Pull on the working
end and the standing part
until the working end is
firmly trapped under the
turn. The knot is now
complete.

Transom Knot

This is similar to a constrictor knot (see page 76). It is used to fix together crossed pieces of rigid material and has a wide range of camping and outdoor uses, for example, to fasten tent poles together and kit to luggage racks. If used as a permanent knot, the ends may be trimmed off for neatness.

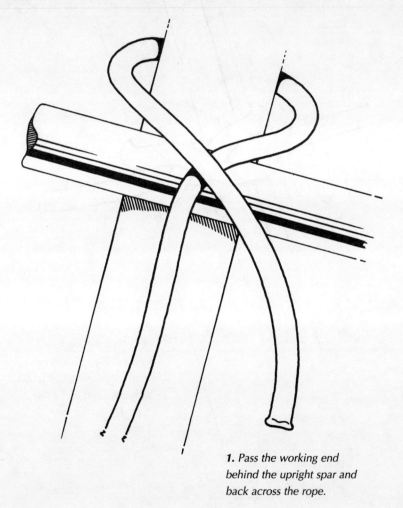

1. Pass the working end behind the upright spar and back across the rope.

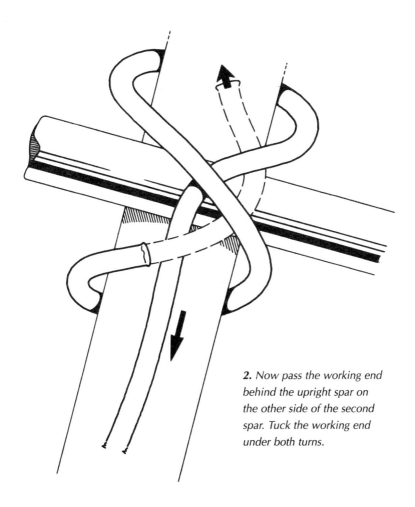

2. Now pass the working end behind the upright spar on the other side of the second spar. Tuck the working end under both turns.

continued on page 82

Transom Knot

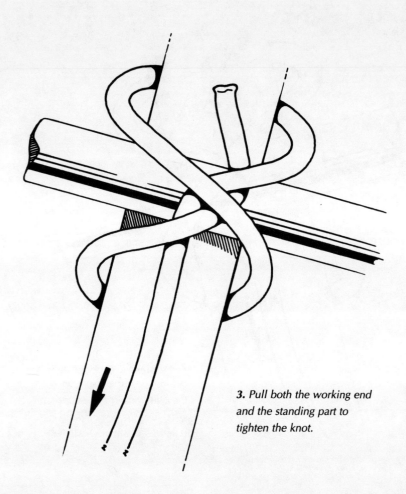

3. Pull both the working end and the standing part to tighten the knot.

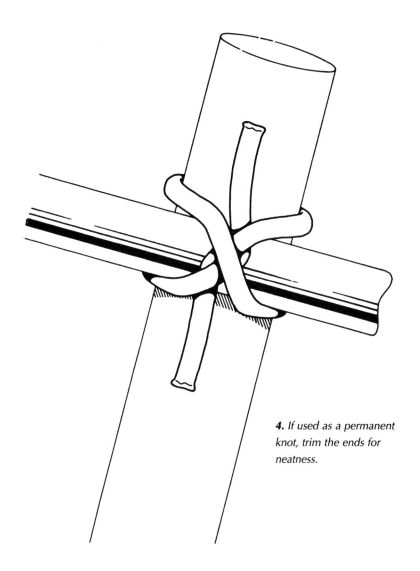

4. If used as a permanent knot, trim the ends for neatness.

PILE HITCH

The pile hitch is a very neat and practical hitch for securing objects to a post. It is ideal as a temporary fixing. The big advantage of this hitch is that it is very easy to tie and release quickly.

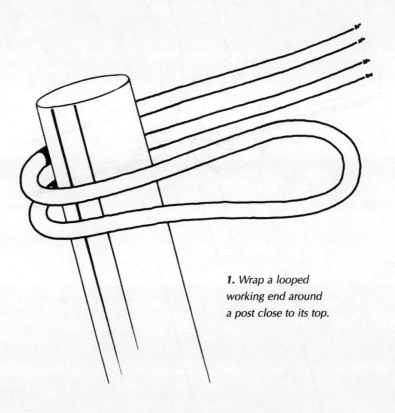

1. Wrap a looped working end around a post close to its top.

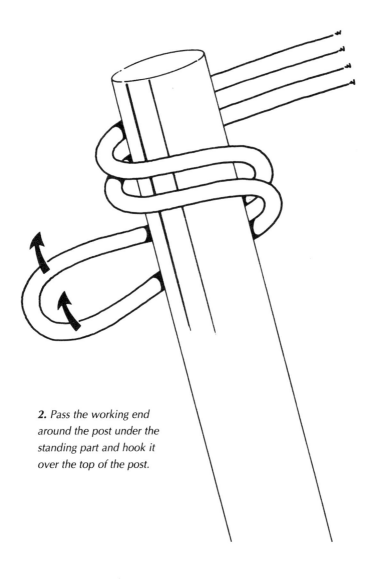

2. Pass the working end around the post under the standing part and hook it over the top of the post.

continued on page 86

Pile Hitch

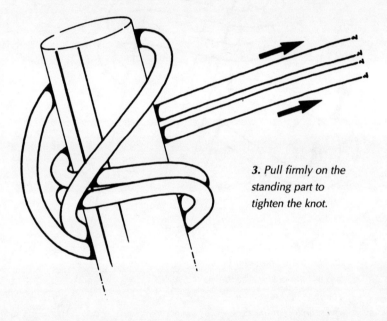

3. Pull firmly on the standing part to tighten the knot.

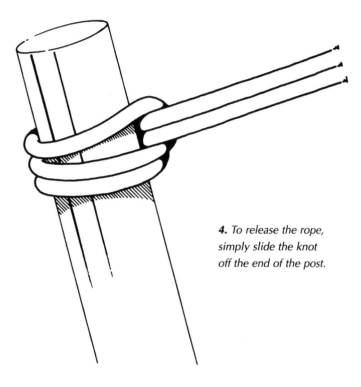

4. To release the rope, simply slide the knot off the end of the post.

Round Turn and Two Half Hitches

This knot is strong, dependable, and when correctly tied, it never jams. This makes it very versatile; you can use it whenever you want to fasten a line to a ring, hook, stake, post, pole, handle, or rail. Once one end of a rope has been secured with a round turn and two half hitches, the other end can be tied with a second knot. This is especially useful for fastening down unwieldy, bulky objects.

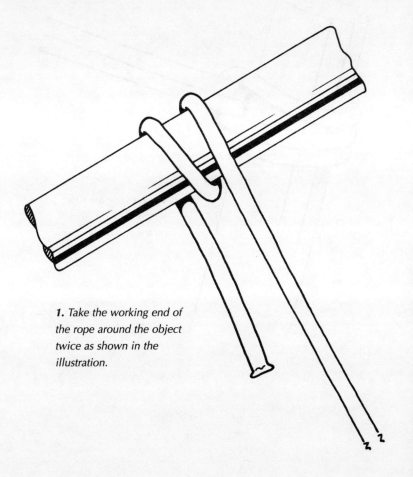

1. Take the working end of the rope around the object twice as shown in the illustration.

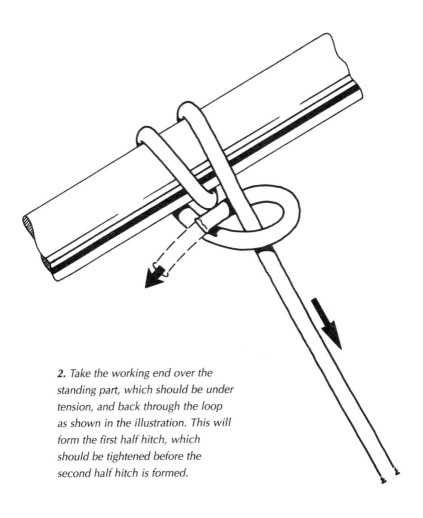

2. Take the working end over the standing part, which should be under tension, and back through the loop as shown in the illustration. This will form the first half hitch, which should be tightened before the second half hitch is formed.

continued on page 90

Round Turn and Two Half Hitches

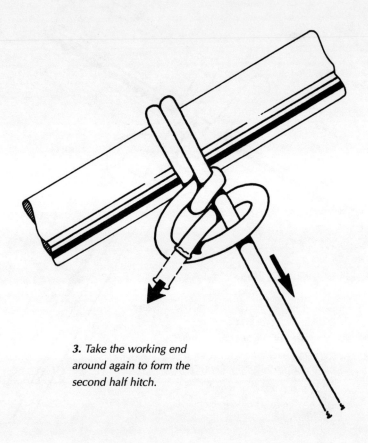

3. Take the working end around again to form the second half hitch.

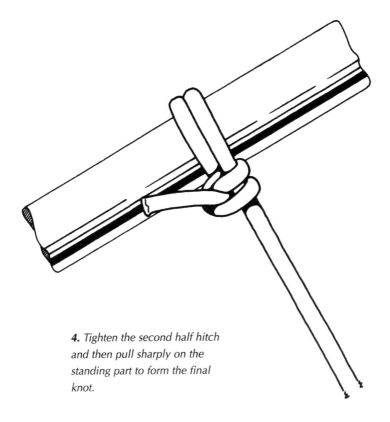

4. *Tighten the second half hitch and then pull sharply on the standing part to form the final knot.*

HIGHWAYMAN'S HITCH

The name of this knot comes from its legendary use by highwaymen and robbers to give them quick release of their horses' reins and so ensure a fast getaway. It is also called the draw hitch.

One pull on the working end and the knot is undone, but the standing end can be put under tension. It is useful for tethering animals, lowering loads, and as a temporary fastening.

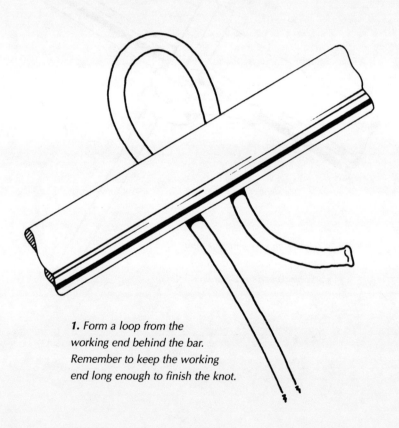

1. Form a loop from the working end behind the bar. Remember to keep the working end long enough to finish the knot.

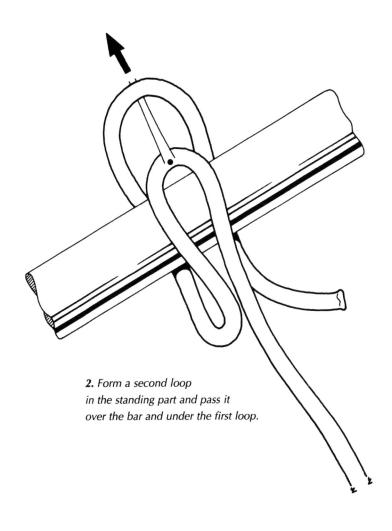

2. Form a second loop
in the standing part and pass it
over the bar and under the first loop.

continued on page 94

Highwayman's Hitch

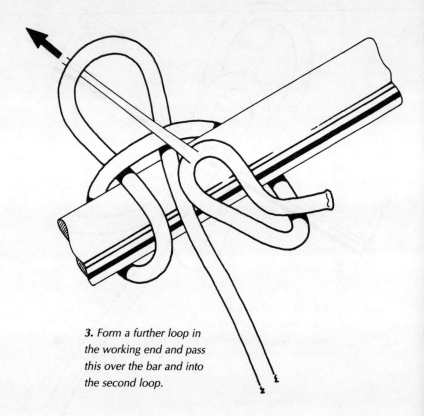

3. Form a further loop in the working end and pass this over the bar and into the second loop.

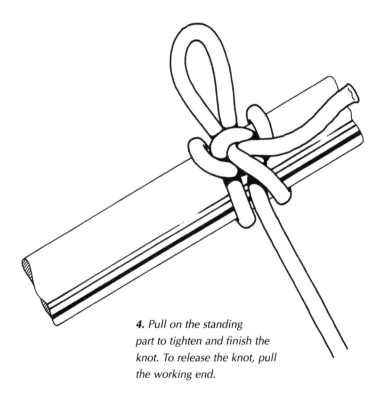

4. Pull on the standing part to tighten and finish the knot. To release the knot, pull the working end.

WAGONER'S HITCH

The wagoner's hitch is a very useful, practical knot that makes it possible to pull tight a line or rope yet leave it ready for immediate release. This makes it an ideal knot for securing loads or deck gear.

Once the line has been heaved tight, it should be secured with at least two half hitches.

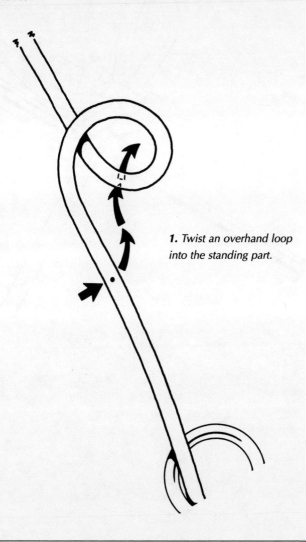

1. Twist an overhand loop into the standing part.

2. *Take hold of the line close to the loop and pass a new loop through it from underneath the line.*

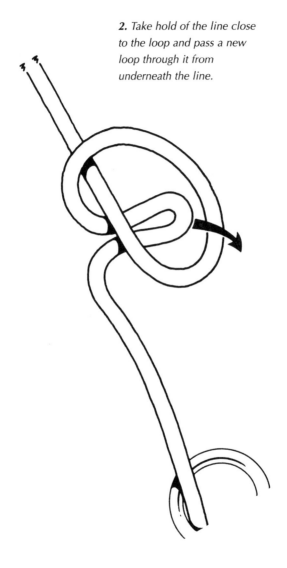

continued on page 98

Wagoner's Hitch

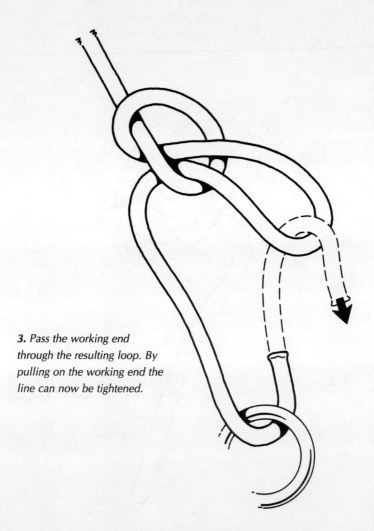

3. Pass the working end through the resulting loop. By pulling on the working end the line can now be tightened.

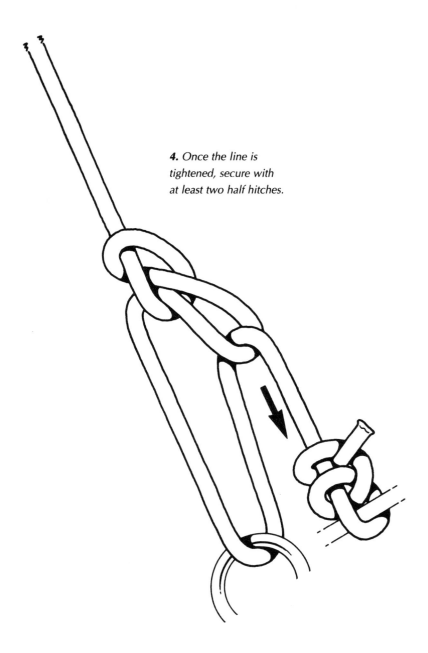

4. Once the line is tightened, secure with at least two half hitches.

TIMBER HITCH

The timber hitch is a temporary noose formed around such objects as tree trunks, planks, and poles so that they can be dragged, pulled, raised, or lowered.

It is made by doubling the working end on itself and twisting it around its own part (not the standing part of the hitch) several times. If the object is very thick, more twists are added. It is a very useful hitch in that it can be quickly put on, is very secure, and does not jam. Unfortunately, it is easy for beginners to tie it incorrectly.

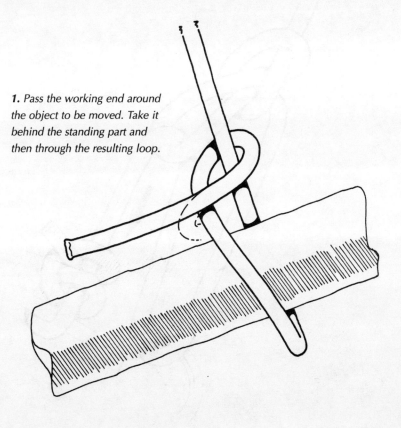

1. Pass the working end around the object to be moved. Take it behind the standing part and then through the resulting loop.

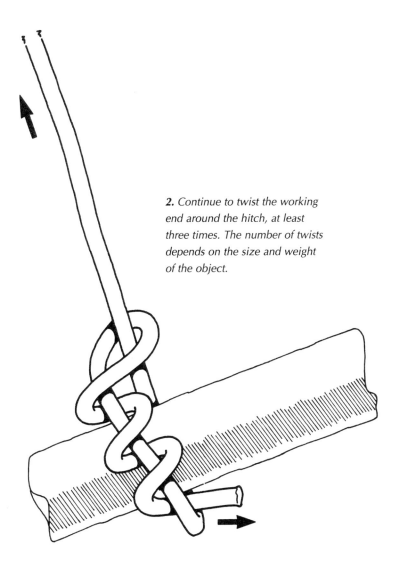

2. Continue to twist the working end around the hitch, at least three times. The number of twists depends on the size and weight of the object.

continued on page 102

Timber Hitch

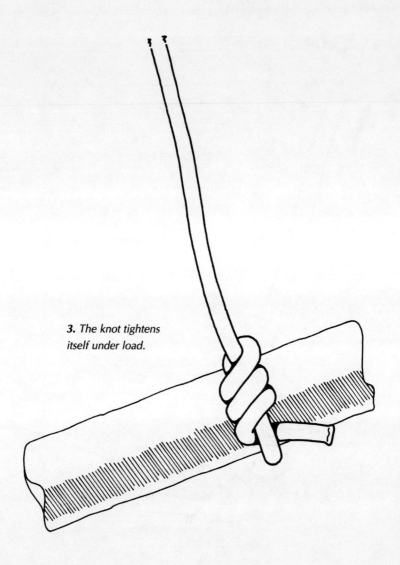

3. *The knot tightens itself under load.*

The **killick hitch** is a variation of the timber hitch specifically used for
dragging and towing. It is created by first tying a timber hitch and then,
some distance down the line, adding a half hitch.

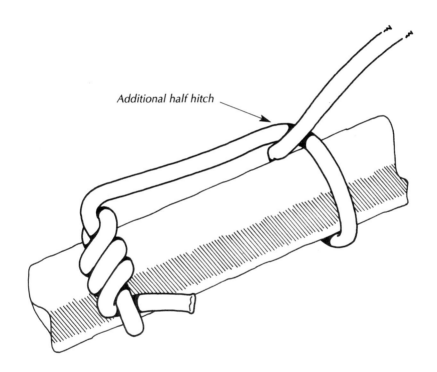

Additional half hitch

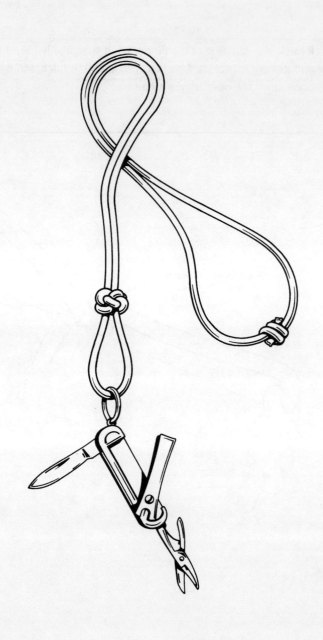

FISHING KNOTS

Camping and fishing have always been closely connected. Camping sites are invariably near streams, rivers, or lakes, so the opportunity to relax with a lazy day's fishing or to catch your supper is never far away. This section contains a collection of the most commonly used fishing knots. Don't forget: An incorrectly tied fishing knot could lose you that fish of a lifetime!

BLOOD KNOT

This knot is a firm favorite with many fishermen and one of the most widely used fishing knots in the world.

It has a relatively high knot strength, with the turns (a minimum of five with each line) helping it absorb strain and shock. It is most effective for joining monofilament lines of the same or similar diameters, but can also be used in many other fishing situations.

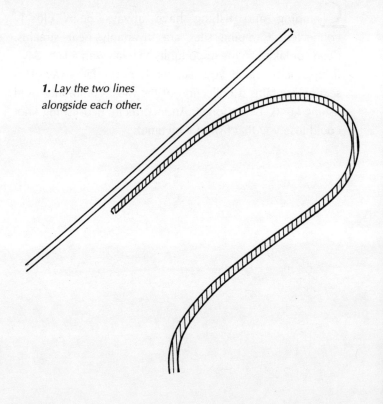

1. Lay the two lines alongside each other.

2. Make four or five turns around one line
and then pass the working end under the
standing part of the same line.

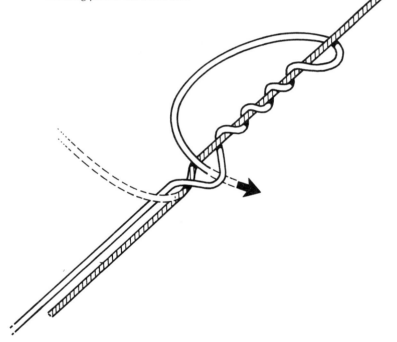

continued on page 108

Blood Knot

3. Repeat the process with the second line.

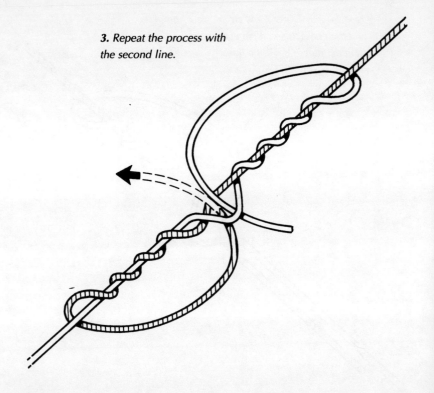

4. Carefully pull the standing parts
to seat and tighten the knot.

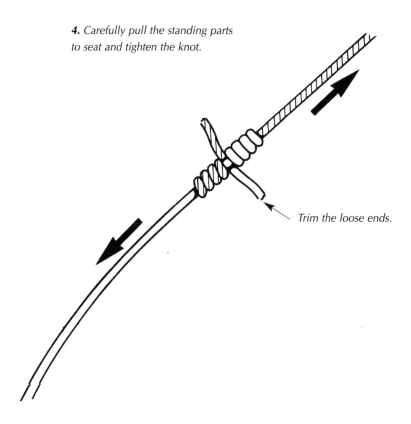

Trim the loose ends.

TUCKED HALF BLOOD KNOT

Also known as the improved clinch knot, this old, tried, and tested knot is a firm favorite with many fishermen. It is very successfully tied with fine monofilament, but when heavier monofilament is used it can prove difficult to draw the knot up tightly.

1. Thread the working end through the eye of the hook and make four or five turns around the standing part.

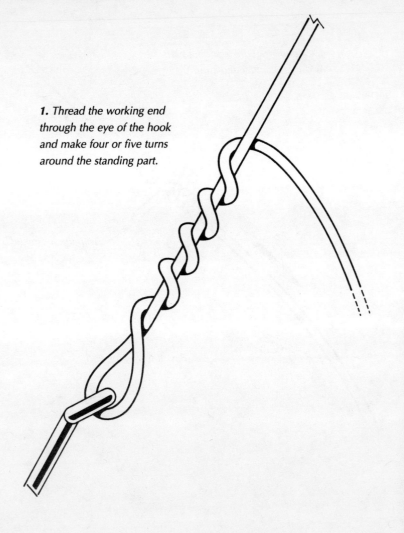

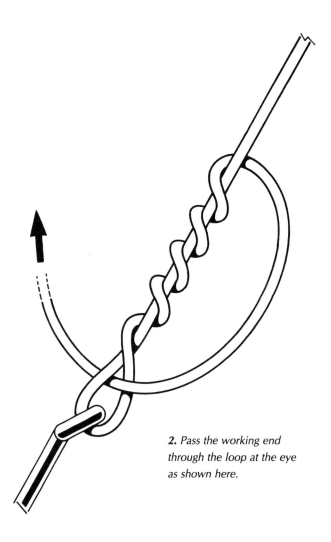

2. Pass the working end
through the loop at the eye
as shown here.

continued on page 112

Tucked Half Blood Knot

3. Pass the working end back through itself. Seat the knot correctly by pulling the standing part and the working end.

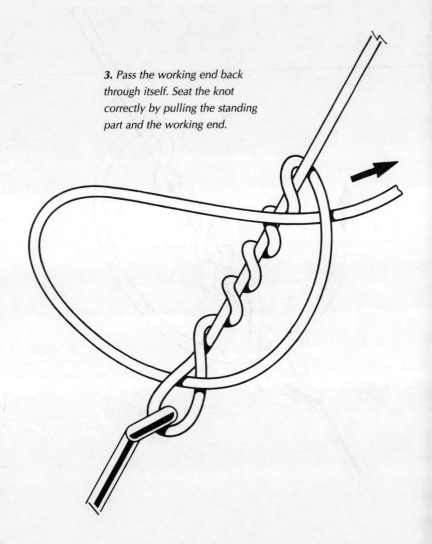

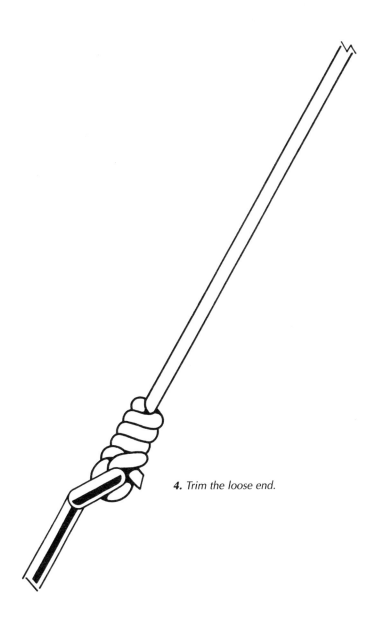

4. Trim the loose end.

DOUBLE LOOP KNOT

The double loop knot, or surgeon's loop, will not slip and can be tied very quickly. It is tied with a single length of line.

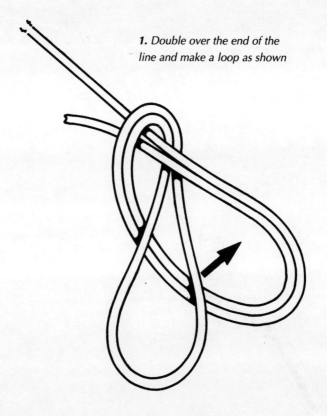

1. Double over the end of the line and make a loop as shown

2. Make two turns around
the line.

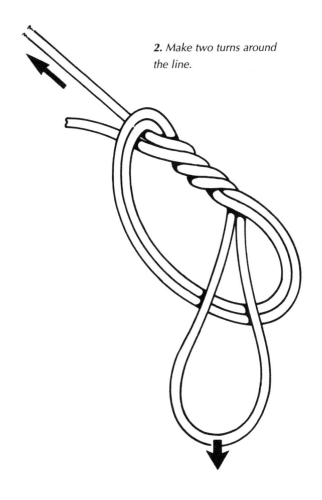

continued on page 116

Double Loop Knot

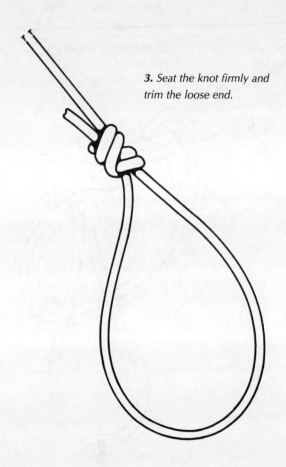

3. *Seat the knot firmly and trim the loose end.*

*Interlocking loops are a quick
and easy method of putting
tackle together.*

SPADE END KNOT

Use this knot to attach hooks with a spade end as opposed to an eyed end. It is important to seat the knot correctly around the hook shank.

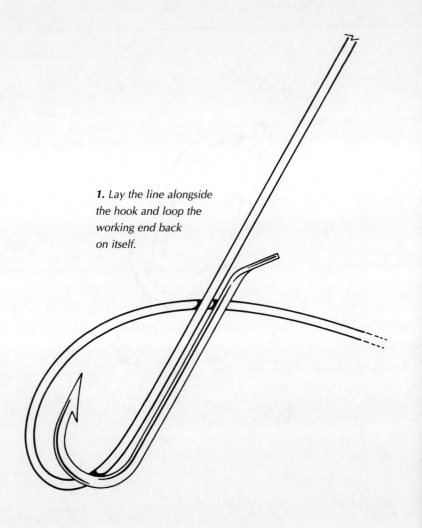

1. Lay the line alongside the hook and loop the working end back on itself.

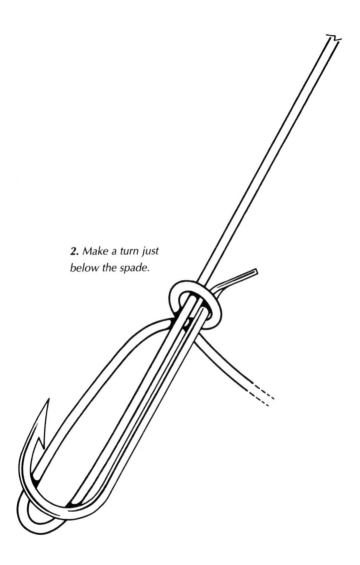

2. *Make a turn just below the spade.*

continued on page 120

Spade End Knot

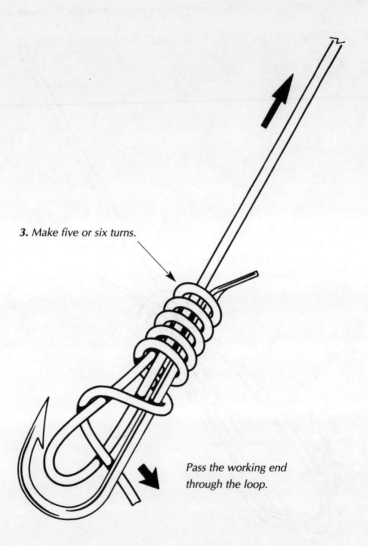

3. Make five or six turns.

Pass the working end through the loop.

4. The knot must be seated correctly just below the spade.

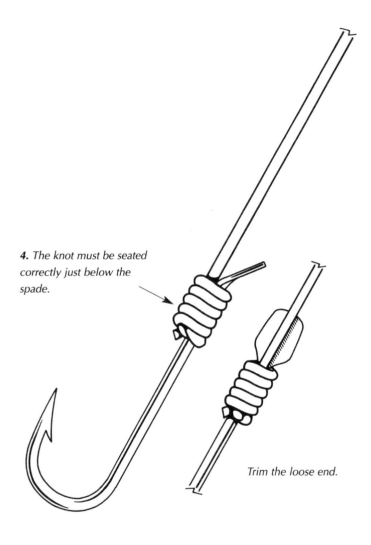

Trim the loose end.

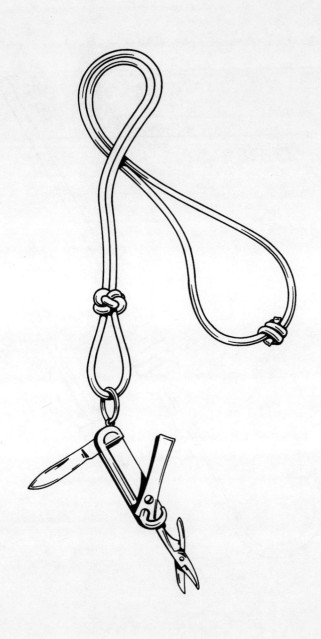

APPLIED KNOTS

Applied knots are knots that are tied to be used for a specific purpose. Often combinations of knots are used to create the required solution. This section contains three very useful examples of applied knots for camping. But remember, with the information contained in this book and a little imagination you can apply many of these camping knots to your next camping trip.

ROPE LADDER

A rope ladder is a great example of how a piece of rope and some knots can create an extremely useful piece of equipment. To tie a ladder of any substantial length is going to require a long piece of rope, so provision for this should be made before starting. A worthwhile exercise is to tie up just one ladder rung as a test to help you estimate the amount of rope that will be required.

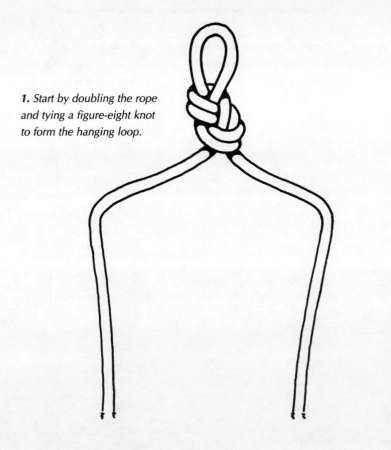

1. Start by doubling the rope and tying a figure-eight knot to form the hanging loop.

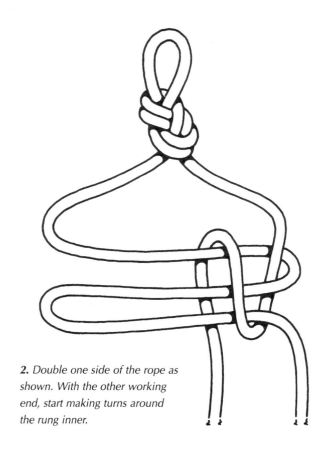

2. Double one side of the rope as shown. With the other working end, start making turns around the rung inner.

continued on page 126

Rope Ladder

3. Make twelve turns, or as many as necessary depending on the width of ladder. Tighten the rung by pulling the standing part and the working end as you finish each one.

Repeat for as many rungs
required. Finish the ladder
at the bottom with
whichever decorative
knot you prefer.

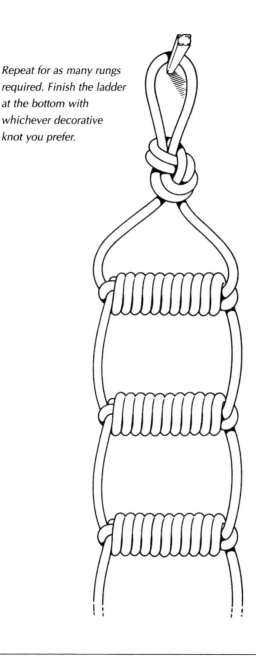

KNIFE LANYARD

A lanyard is usually worn around the neck or attached to a belt for the purpose of holding a wide variety of objects. Even though its technical name is the knife lanyard knot, it is also regularly used for holding whistles, watches, and binoculars. Because the knot is left in view, its very decorative appearance is a great asset.

It may help to create the first two steps around your hand, as shown in the illustration.

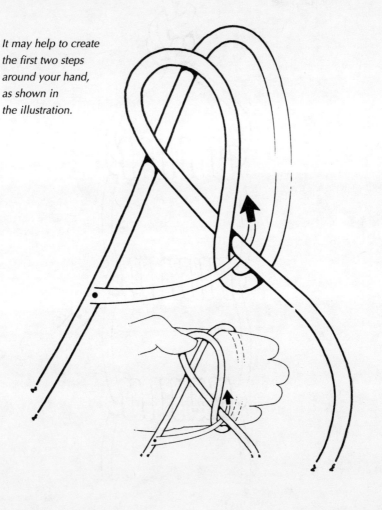

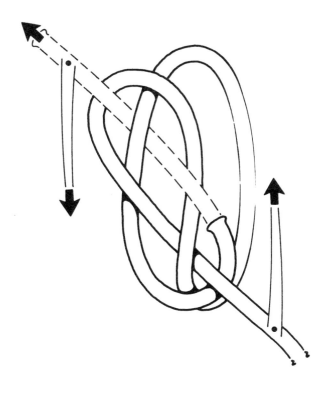

continued on page 130

Knife Lanyard

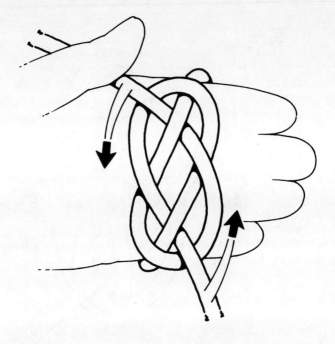

At this point, the knot should look like this, with the pattern on the front and the main loop running behind your hand.

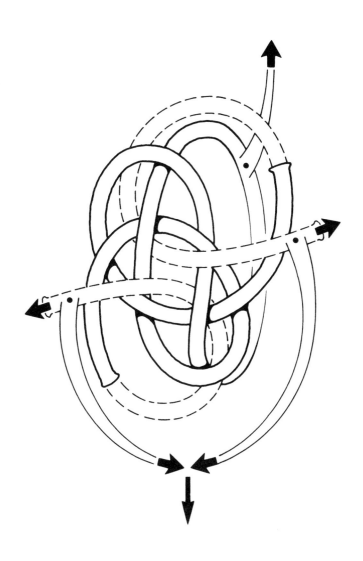

continued on page 132

Knife Lanyard

Slowly draw the knot together, working it into its final shape.

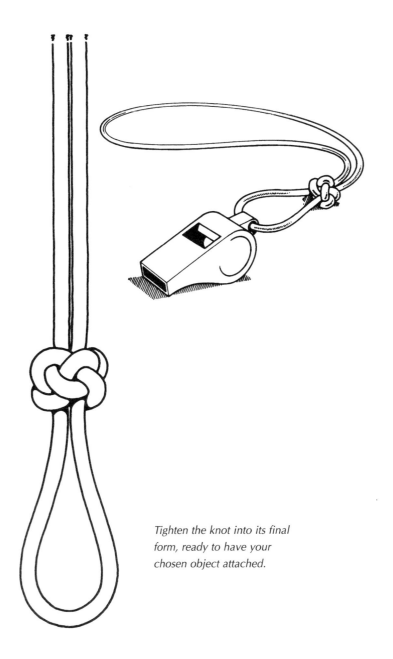

Tighten the knot into its final form, ready to have your chosen object attached.

BARREL SLING

This applied knot is specifically designed to hold a cylindrical container or object. It is particularly useful for suspending open containers off the ground. It can be used for cooking purposes as long as it is tied with thin wire and not rope.

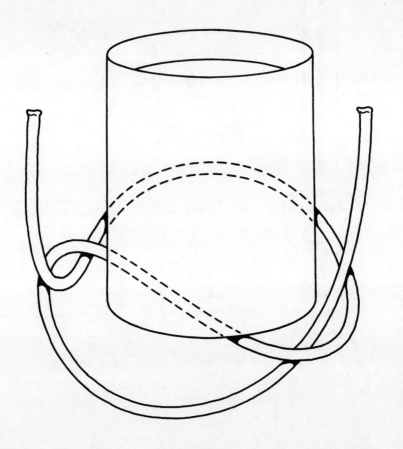

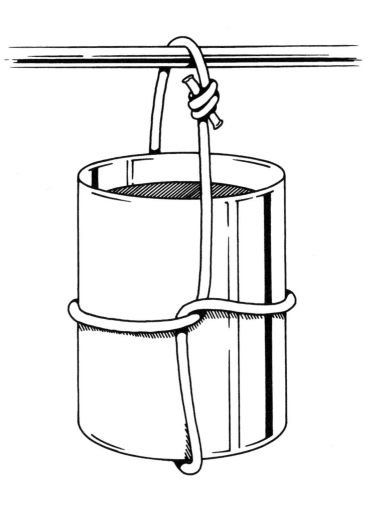

GLOSSARY

Bend. The action of tying two ropes together by their ends. Also the name given to the group of knots that are used to tie lines to each other or to some other object.

Bight. The slack section of the rope between the working end and the standing end. The term is particularly used when this section of the rope is formed into a loop or turned back on itself. Knots tied "in the bight" or "on the bight" do not require you to use the ends in the tying process.

Braid. To interweave several strands.

Breaking strength or strain. The manufacturer's estimate of the load that will cause a rope to part. This calculation is based on strength of a dry line under a steady pull; it generally takes no account of wetness, wear and tear, knots, or shock loading. Lines are weaker when worn, wet, or knotted; the manufacturer's estimate cannot, therefore, be regarded as a safe working load.

Cable-laid. Rope formed of three right-handed hawsers laid up left-handed to make a larger, nine-stranded rope or cable.

Cord. The name given to several tightly twisted yarns making a line with a diameter of less than 1/2 inch.

Cordage. Collective name for ropes and cords; especially used to describe the ropes in a ship's rigging.

Core. The inner, or central, part found in ropes and sinnets of more than three strands, and in most braided lines. Formed from a bundle of parallel strands or loosely twisted yarn running the length of the rope, or the central part of a monkey's fist knot, inserted to add weight.

Eye. A circle or loop attached or formed at the end of a hook or item of tackle, to which line is attached or a loop formed at the end of a length of rope.

Fray. To unravel, especially the end of a piece of rope.

Hitch. Knot made to secure a rope to a ring, spar, etc., or to another rope.

Lanyard. A short length of rope or cord made decorative with knots and sinnets. Used to secure personal objects; usually worn around the neck or attached to a belt.

Lay. The direction, right- or left-handed, of the twist in the strands that form a rope.

Line. Generic name for cordage with no specific purpose, although it can describe a particular use (clothesline, fishing line, etc.).

Loop. Part of a rope that is bent so that it comes together across itself.

Monofilament. Strong and flexible single-strand nylon line.

Nip. The binding pressure within a knot that stops it from slipping.

Plain-laid rope. Three-strand rope laid (twisted) to the right.

Rope. Strong, thick cord more than 1 inch in circumference made from twisted strands of fiber, wire, etc.

Seat or Seated. A term used to describe the process of knot formation.

Small stuff. Thin cordage, twine, string, rope, or line that has a circumference of less than 1 inch, or a diameter of less than 1/2 inch.

Spade end. The flattened end of the shank of a hook.

Splice. To join the ends of rope by interweaving the strands.

Standing end. The short area at the end of the standing part of the rope.

Standing part. The part of the rope that is fixed and under tension (as opposed to the free working end with which the knot is tied).

Stopper knot. Any terminal knot used to bind the end of a line, cord, or rope to prevent it from unraveling and also to provide a decorative end.

Strand. Yarns twisted together in the opposite direction to the yarn itself. Rope made from strands (rope that is not braided) is called laid line.

Turn. One complete revolution of one line around another.

Twine. Thin line of various types for various uses, as in whipping twine, etc.

Working end. The part of the rope or cord used actively in tying a knot. The opposite of the standing end.

Yarn. The basic element of rope or cord formed from artificial or synthetic filaments or natural fibers.

Conversion Chart

Note: These conversion factors are not exact. They are given only to the accuracy you're likely to need in everyday calculations.

Linear Measure

0.25 inch	= 0.6 cm
0.5 inch	= 1.25 cm
1 inch	= 2.54 cm
2 inches	= 5.08 cm
4 inches	= 10.16 cm
6 inches	= 15.25 cm
8 inches	= 20.32 cm
10 inches	= 25.40 cm
12 inches (1 foot)	= 30.48 cm
2 feet	= 0.61 m
3 feet (1 yard)	= 0.91 m
5 feet	= 1.52 m
10 feet	= 3.05 m

Measures of Weight

1 lb	= 450 g
2 lb	= 900 g
5 lb	= 2.25 kg
10 lb	= 4.5 kg
20 lb	= 9 kg
50 lb	= 23 kg
100 lb	= 46 kg

Temperature

Celsius	Fahrenheit
-17.8°	= 0°
-10°	= 14°
0°	= 32°
10°	= 50°
20°	= 68°
30°	= 86°
40°	= 104°
50°	= 122°
60°	= 140°
70°	= 158°
80°	= 176°
90°	= 194°
100°	= 212°

INDEX OF KNOTS